ASA-SP-57

The Standard Pilot Log
SP-57

© 1991–2014 Aviation Supplies & Academics, Inc.

ASA-SP-57
ISBN 1-56027-330-5
978-1-56027-330-1

All rights reserved.
Reproduction or use, without express permission,
in any manner, is prohibited.

Published by
Aviation Supplies & Academics, Inc.
7005 132nd Place SE
Newcastle, WA 98059-3153
Website: www.asa2fly.com
Email: asa@asa2fly.com

Printed in the United States of America

The Standard Pilot Log

Name _____

Permanent Mailing Address _____

_____

Logbook Number _____

From _____

To _____

Certificates Held

Type	Date Issued	Certificate Number
STUDENT PILOT	_____	_____
SPORT PILOT	_____	_____
RECREATIONAL PILOT	_____	_____
PRIVATE PILOT	_____	_____
COMMERCIAL PILOT	_____	_____
FLIGHT INSTRUCTOR	_____	_____
AIRLINE TRANSPORT PILOT	_____	_____
AVIATION TECHNICIAN	_____	_____
GROUND INSTRUCTOR	_____	_____
_____	_____	_____
_____	_____	_____

Rating Record

- ☐ AIRPLANE
- ☐ SINGLE ENGINE: ☐ LAND   ☐ SEA
- ☐ MULTI-ENGINE: ☐ LAND   ☐ SEA
- ☐ MULTI-ENGINE: Limited to Center Line Thrust
- ☐ INSTRUMENT
- ☐ GLIDER   ☐ AERO TOW   ☐ WINCH TOW
- ☐ POWERED PARACHUTE   ☐ WEIGHT-SHIFT CONTROL
- ☐ ROTORCRAFT   ☐ HELICOPTER   ☐ GYROPLANE
- ☐ LIGHTER-THAN-AIR   ☐ AIRSHIP   ☐ BALLOON
- ☐ POWERED LIFT
- ☐ GI BASIC   ☐ GI ADVANCED   ☐ GI INSTRUMENT
- ☐ OTHER RATINGS (Specify)

_____

Aircraft Type Ratings

_____
_____
_____
_____
_____
_____
_____
_____
_____
_____
_____
_____

YEAR 20___ DATE	AIRCRAFT MAKE and MODEL	AIRCRAFT IDENTIFCATION NUMBER	POINTS OF DEPARTURE & ARRIVAL		AIRCRAFT CATEGORY and CLASSIFICATION					TYPE OF PILOTING TIME			
			FROM	TO	AIRPLANE SINGLE ENGINE LAND	AIRPLANE MULTI-ENGINE LAND	ROTORCRAFT HELICOPTER			DUAL RECEIVED	PILOT-IN-COMMAND	SECOND-IN-COMMAND	AS FLIGHT INSTRUCTOR
			PAGE TOTAL										
			AMOUNT FORWARD										
			TOTAL TO DATE										

GROUND TRAINER	CONDITIONS OF FLIGHT						NO. INSTR. APPR.	NO. LDG. DAY/NIGHT	TOTAL DURATION OF FLIGHT	REMARKS PROCEDURES, MANEUVERS, ENDORSEMENTS
	DAY	NIGHT		CROSS-COUNTRY	ACTUAL INSTRUMENT	SIMULATED INSTRUMENT				
										I certify that the statements made by me on this form are true.
										PILOT'S SIGNATURE

YEAR 20___ DATE	AIRCRAFT MAKE and MODEL	AIRCRAFT IDENTIFCATION NUMBER	POINTS OF DEPARTURE & ARRIVAL		AIRCRAFT CATEGORY and CLASSIFICATION						TYPE OF PILOTING TIME				
			FROM	TO	AIRPLANE SINGLE ENGINE LAND	AIRPLANE MULTI-ENGINE LAND	ROTORCRAFT HELICOPTER				DUAL RECEIVED	PILOT-IN-COMMAND	SECOND-IN-COMMAND		AS FLIGHT INSTRUCTOR
			PAGE TOTAL												
			AMOUNT FORWARD												
			TOTAL TO DATE												

GROUND TRAINER	CONDITIONS OF FLIGHT						NO. INSTR. APPR.	NO. LDG.		TOTAL DURATION OF FLIGHT		REMARKS PROCEDURES, MANEUVERS, ENDORSEMENTS
	DAY	NIGHT		CROSS-COUNTRY	ACTUAL INSTRUMENT	SIMULATED INSTRUMENT		DAY	NIGHT			
												I certify that the statements made by me on this form are true.
												PILOT'S SIGNATURE

YEAR 20___ DATE	AIRCRAFT MAKE and MODEL	AIRCRAFT IDENTIFCATION NUMBER	POINTS OF DEPARTURE & ARRIVAL		AIRCRAFT CATEGORY and CLASSIFICATION				TYPE OF PILOTING TIME			
			FROM	TO	AIRPLANE SINGLE ENGINE LAND	AIRPLANE MULTI-ENGINE LAND	ROTORCRAFT HELICOPTER		DUAL RECEIVED	PILOT-IN-COMMAND	SECOND-IN-COMMAND	AS FLIGHT INSTRUCTOR
			PAGE TOTAL									
			AMOUNT FORWARD									
			TOTAL TO DATE									

GROUND TRAINER	CONDITIONS OF FLIGHT						NO. INSTR. APPR.	NO. LDG. DAY / NIGHT	TOTAL DURATION OF FLIGHT		REMARKS PROCEDURES, MANEUVERS, ENDORSEMENTS
	DAY	NIGHT		CROSS-COUNTRY	ACTUAL INSTRUMENT	SIMULATED INSTRUMENT					
											I certify that the statements made by me on this form are true.
											PILOT'S SIGNATURE

YEAR 20__ DATE	AIRCRAFT MAKE and MODEL	AIRCRAFT IDENTIFCATION NUMBER	POINTS OF DEPARTURE & ARRIVAL		AIRCRAFT CATEGORY and CLASSIFICATION				TYPE OF PILOTING TIME			
			FROM	TO	AIRPLANE SINGLE ENGINE LAND	AIRPLANE MULTI-ENGINE LAND	ROTORCRAFT HELICOPTER		DUAL RECEIVED	PILOT-IN-COMMAND	SECOND-IN-COMMAND	AS FLIGHT INSTRUCTOR
				PAGE TOTAL								
				AMOUNT FORWARD								
				TOTAL TO DATE								

GROUND TRAINER	CONDITIONS OF FLIGHT						NO. INSTR. APPR.	NO. LDG. DAY/NIGHT	TOTAL DURATION OF FLIGHT		REMARKS PROCEDURES, MANEUVERS, ENDORSEMENTS
	DAY	NIGHT	CROSS-COUNTRY	ACTUAL INSTRUMENT	SIMULATED INSTRUMENT						
											I certify that the statements made by me on this form are true.
											PILOT'S SIGNATURE

YEAR 20___ DATE	AIRCRAFT MAKE and MODEL	AIRCRAFT IDENTIFCATION NUMBER	POINTS OF DEPARTURE & ARRIVAL		AIRCRAFT CATEGORY and CLASSIFICATION						TYPE OF PILOTING TIME							
			FROM	TO	AIRPLANE SINGLE ENGINE LAND		AIRPLANE MULTI-ENGINE LAND		ROTORCRAFT HELICOPTER				DUAL RECEIVED		PILOT-IN-COMMAND		SECOND-IN-COMMAND		AS FLIGHT INSTRUCTOR
			PAGE TOTAL																
			AMOUNT FORWARD																
			TOTAL TO DATE																

GROUND TRAINER	CONDITIONS OF FLIGHT						NO. INSTR. APPR.	NO. LDG. DAY/NIGHT	TOTAL DURATION OF FLIGHT	REMARKS PROCEDURES, MANEUVERS, ENDORSEMENTS
	DAY		NIGHT		CROSS-COUNTRY		ACTUAL INSTRUMENT		SIMULATED INSTRUMENT	
										I certify that the statements made by me on this form are true.
										PILOT'S SIGNATURE

YEAR 20__ DATE	AIRCRAFT MAKE and MODEL	AIRCRAFT IDENTIFCATION NUMBER	POINTS OF DEPARTURE & ARRIVAL		AIRCRAFT CATEGORY and CLASSIFICATION							TYPE OF PILOTING TIME								
			FROM	TO	AIRPLANE SINGLE ENGINE LAND		AIRPLANE MULTI-ENGINE LAND		ROTORCRAFT HELICOPTER			DUAL RECEIVED		PILOT-IN-COMMAND		SECOND-IN-COMMAND		AS FLIGHT INSTRUCTOR	
			PAGE TOTAL																	
			AMOUNT FORWARD																	
			TOTAL TO DATE																	

GROUND TRAINER	CONDITIONS OF FLIGHT						NO. INSTR. APPR.	NO. LDG. DAY/NIGHT	TOTAL DURATION OF FLIGHT	REMARKS PROCEDURES, MANEUVERS, ENDORSEMENTS
	DAY	NIGHT	CROSS-COUNTRY	ACTUAL INSTRUMENT	SIMULATED INSTRUMENT					
										I certify that the statements made by me on this form are true.
										PILOT'S SIGNATURE

YEAR 20__ DATE	AIRCRAFT MAKE and MODEL	AIRCRAFT IDENTIFCATION NUMBER	POINTS OF DEPARTURE & ARRIVAL		AIRCRAFT CATEGORY and CLASSIFICATION				TYPE OF PILOTING TIME			
			FROM	TO	AIRPLANE SINGLE ENGINE LAND	AIRPLANE MULTI-ENGINE LAND	ROTORCRAFT HELICOPTER		DUAL RECEIVED	PILOT-IN-COMMAND	SECOND-IN-COMMAND	AS FLIGHT INSTRUCTOR
				PAGE TOTAL								
				AMOUNT FORWARD								
				TOTAL TO DATE								

GROUND TRAINER	CONDITIONS OF FLIGHT						NO. INSTR. APPR.	NO. LDG. DAY / NIGHT	TOTAL DURATION OF FLIGHT		REMARKS PROCEDURES, MANEUVERS, ENDORSEMENTS
	DAY		NIGHT		CROSS-COUNTRY	ACTUAL INSTRUMENT	SIMULATED INSTRUMENT				
											I certify that the statements made by me on this form are true.
											PILOT'S SIGNATURE

YEAR 20___ DATE	AIRCRAFT MAKE and MODEL	AIRCRAFT IDENTIFCATION NUMBER	POINTS OF DEPARTURE & ARRIVAL		AIRCRAFT CATEGORY and CLASSIFICATION					TYPE OF PILOTING TIME							
			FROM	TO	AIRPLANE SINGLE ENGINE LAND		AIRPLANE MULTI-ENGINE LAND		ROTORCRAFT HELICOPTER				DUAL RECEIVED		PILOT-IN-COMMAND		SECOND-IN-COMMAND		AS FLIGHT INSTRUCTOR	
				PAGE TOTAL																	
				AMOUNT FORWARD																	
				TOTAL TO DATE																	

GROUND TRAINER	CONDITIONS OF FLIGHT						NO. INSTR. APPR.	NO. LDG. DAY / NIGHT	TOTAL DURATION OF FLIGHT		REMARKS PROCEDURES, MANEUVERS, ENDORSEMENTS
	DAY	NIGHT	CROSS-COUNTRY	ACTUAL INSTRUMENT	SIMULATED INSTRUMENT						
											I certify that the statements made by me on this form are true.
											PILOT'S SIGNATURE

YEAR 20__ DATE	AIRCRAFT MAKE and MODEL	AIRCRAFT IDENTIFCATION NUMBER	POINTS OF DEPARTURE & ARRIVAL		AIRCRAFT CATEGORY and CLASSIFICATION					TYPE OF PILOTING TIME							
			FROM	TO	AIRPLANE SINGLE ENGINE LAND		AIRPLANE MULTI-ENGINE LAND		ROTORCRAFT HELICOPTER				DUAL RECEIVED		PILOT-IN-COMMAND	SECOND-IN-COMMAND	AS FLIGHT INSTRUCTOR
				PAGE TOTAL													
				AMOUNT FORWARD													
				TOTAL TO DATE													

GROUND TRAINER	CONDITIONS OF FLIGHT						NO. INSTR. APPR.	NO. LDG. DAY / NIGHT	TOTAL DURATION OF FLIGHT		REMARKS PROCEDURES, MANEUVERS, ENDORSEMENTS
	DAY	NIGHT	CROSS-COUNTRY	ACTUAL INSTRUMENT	SIMULATED INSTRUMENT						
											I certify that the statements made by me on this form are true.
											PILOT'S SIGNATURE

YEAR 20___ DATE	AIRCRAFT MAKE and MODEL	AIRCRAFT IDENTIFCATION NUMBER	POINTS OF DEPARTURE & ARRIVAL		AIRCRAFT CATEGORY and CLASSIFICATION					TYPE OF PILOTING TIME							
			FROM	TO	AIRPLANE SINGLE ENGINE LAND		AIRPLANE MULTI-ENGINE LAND		ROTORCRAFT HELICOPTER		DUAL RECEIVED		PILOT-IN-COMMAND		SECOND-IN-COMMAND		AS FLIGHT INSTRUCTOR
			PAGE TOTAL														
			AMOUNT FORWARD														
			TOTAL TO DATE														

GROUND TRAINER	CONDITIONS OF FLIGHT						NO. INSTR. APPR.	NO. LDG. DAY/NIGHT	TOTAL DURATION OF FLIGHT	REMARKS PROCEDURES, MANEUVERS, ENDORSEMENTS
	DAY	NIGHT		CROSS-COUNTRY	ACTUAL INSTRUMENT	SIMULATED INSTRUMENT				
									I certify that the statements made by me on this form are true.
										PILOT'S SIGNATURE

YEAR 20__ DATE	AIRCRAFT MAKE and MODEL	AIRCRAFT IDENTIFCATION NUMBER	POINTS OF DEPARTURE & ARRIVAL		AIRCRAFT CATEGORY and CLASSIFICATION					TYPE OF PILOTING TIME							
			FROM	TO	AIRPLANE SINGLE ENGINE LAND		AIRPLANE MULTI-ENGINE LAND		ROTORCRAFT HELICOPTER				DUAL RECEIVED		PILOT-IN- COMMAND		SECOND-IN- COMMAND		AS FLIGHT INSTRUCTOR	
			PAGE TOTAL																	
			AMOUNT FORWARD																	
			TOTAL TO DATE																	

GROUND TRAINER	CONDITIONS OF FLIGHT						NO. INSTR. APPR.	NO. LDG. DAY/NIGHT	TOTAL DURATION OF FLIGHT		REMARKS PROCEDURES, MANEUVERS, ENDORSEMENTS
	DAY		NIGHT		CROSS-COUNTRY		ACTUAL INSTRUMENT		SIMULATED INSTRUMENT		
											I certify that the statements made by me on this form are true.
											PILOT'S SIGNATURE

YEAR 20___ DATE	AIRCRAFT MAKE and MODEL	AIRCRAFT IDENTIFCATION NUMBER	POINTS OF DEPARTURE & ARRIVAL		AIRCRAFT CATEGORY and CLASSIFICATION					TYPE OF PILOTING TIME												
			FROM	TO	AIRPLANE SINGLE ENGINE LAND		AIRPLANE MULTI-ENGINE LAND		ROTORCRAFT HELICOPTER				DUAL RECEIVED			PILOT-IN-COMMAND			SECOND-IN-COMMAND			AS FLIGHT INSTRUCTOR
				PAGE TOTAL																		
				AMOUNT FORWARD																		
				TOTAL TO DATE																		

GROUND TRAINER	CONDITIONS OF FLIGHT						NO. INSTR. APPR.	NO. LDG. DAY/NIGHT	TOTAL DURATION OF FLIGHT		REMARKS PROCEDURES, MANEUVERS, ENDORSEMENTS
	DAY		NIGHT		CROSS-COUNTRY		ACTUAL INSTRUMENT		SIMULATED INSTRUMENT		
													I certify that the statements made by me on this form are true.
													PILOT'S SIGNATURE

YEAR 20___ DATE	AIRCRAFT MAKE and MODEL	AIRCRAFT IDENTIFCATION NUMBER	POINTS OF DEPARTURE & ARRIVAL		AIRCRAFT CATEGORY and CLASSIFICATION					TYPE OF PILOTING TIME			
			FROM	TO	AIRPLANE SINGLE ENGINE LAND	AIRPLANE MULTI-ENGINE LAND	ROTORCRAFT HELICOPTER			DUAL RECEIVED	PILOT-IN-COMMAND	SECOND-IN-COMMAND	AS FLIGHT INSTRUCTOR
			PAGE TOTAL										
			AMOUNT FORWARD										
			TOTAL TO DATE										

GROUND TRAINER	CONDITIONS OF FLIGHT						NO. INSTR. APPR.	NO. LDG. DAY/NIGHT	TOTAL DURATION OF FLIGHT		REMARKS PROCEDURES, MANEUVERS, ENDORSEMENTS
	DAY	NIGHT	CROSS-COUNTRY	ACTUAL INSTRUMENT	SIMULATED INSTRUMENT						
											I certify that the statements made by me on this form are true.
											PILOT'S SIGNATURE

YEAR 20___ DATE	AIRCRAFT MAKE and MODEL	AIRCRAFT IDENTIFCATION NUMBER	POINTS OF DEPARTURE & ARRIVAL		AIRCRAFT CATEGORY and CLASSIFICATION					TYPE OF PILOTING TIME								
			FROM	TO	AIRPLANE SINGLE ENGINE LAND		AIRPLANE MULTI-ENGINE LAND		ROTORCRAFT HELICOPTER				DUAL RECEIVED		PILOT-IN-COMMAND		SECOND-IN-COMMAND	AS FLIGHT INSTRUCTOR
			PAGE TOTAL															
			AMOUNT FORWARD															
			TOTAL TO DATE															

GROUND TRAINER	CONDITIONS OF FLIGHT						NO. INSTR. APPR.	NO. LDG. DAY/NIGHT	TOTAL DURATION OF FLIGHT	REMARKS PROCEDURES, MANEUVERS, ENDORSEMENTS
	DAY		NIGHT		CROSS-COUNTRY	ACTUAL INSTRUMENT	SIMULATED INSTRUMENT				
											I certify that the statements made by me on this form are true.
											PILOT'S SIGNATURE

YEAR 20__ DATE	AIRCRAFT MAKE and MODEL	AIRCRAFT IDENTIFCATION NUMBER	POINTS OF DEPARTURE & ARRIVAL		AIRCRAFT CATEGORY and CLASSIFICATION					TYPE OF PILOTING TIME							
			FROM	TO	AIRPLANE SINGLE ENGINE LAND	AIRPLANE MULTI-ENGINE LAND	ROTORCRAFT HELICOPTER			DUAL RECEIVED		PILOT-IN-COMMAND		SECOND-IN-COMMAND		AS FLIGHT INSTRUCTOR	
				PAGE TOTAL													
				AMOUNT FORWARD													
				TOTAL TO DATE													

GROUND TRAINER		CONDITIONS OF FLIGHT								NO. INSTR. APPR.	NO. LDG. DAY/NIGHT	TOTAL DURATION OF FLIGHT		REMARKS PROCEDURES, MANEUVERS, ENDORSEMENTS
		DAY		NIGHT		CROSS-COUNTRY		ACTUAL INSTRUMENT	SIMULATED INSTRUMENT					
														I certify that the statements made by me on this form are true.
														PILOT'S SIGNATURE

YEAR 20___ DATE	AIRCRAFT MAKE and MODEL	AIRCRAFT IDENTIFCATION NUMBER	POINTS OF DEPARTURE & ARRIVAL		AIRCRAFT CATEGORY and CLASSIFICATION							TYPE OF PILOTING TIME								
			FROM	TO	AIRPLANE SINGLE ENGINE LAND		AIRPLANE MULTI-ENGINE LAND		ROTORCRAFT HELICOPTER				DUAL RECEIVED		PILOT-IN-COMMAND		SECOND-IN-COMMAND		AS FLIGHT INSTRUCTOR	
			PAGE TOTAL																	
			AMOUNT FORWARD																	
			TOTAL TO DATE																	

GROUND TRAINER	CONDITIONS OF FLIGHT						NO. INSTR. APPR.	NO. LDG. DAY/NIGHT	TOTAL DURATION OF FLIGHT	REMARKS PROCEDURES, MANEUVERS, ENDORSEMENTS
	DAY	NIGHT	CROSS-COUNTRY	ACTUAL INSTRUMENT	SIMULATED INSTRUMENT					
									I certify that the statements made by me on this form are true.
										PILOT'S SIGNATURE

YEAR 20___ DATE	AIRCRAFT MAKE and MODEL	AIRCRAFT IDENTIFCATION NUMBER	POINTS OF DEPARTURE & ARRIVAL		AIRCRAFT CATEGORY and CLASSIFICATION					TYPE OF PILOTING TIME								
			FROM	TO	AIRPLANE SINGLE ENGINE LAND		AIRPLANE MULTI-ENGINE LAND		ROTORCRAFT HELICOPTER				DUAL RECEIVED		PILOT-IN-COMMAND		SECOND-IN-COMMAND		AS FLIGHT INSTRUCTOR	
			PAGE TOTAL																	
			AMOUNT FORWARD																	
			TOTAL TO DATE																	

GROUND TRAINER	CONDITIONS OF FLIGHT						NO. INSTR. APPR.	NO. LDG. DAY / NIGHT	TOTAL DURATION OF FLIGHT		REMARKS PROCEDURES, MANEUVERS, ENDORSEMENTS
	DAY	NIGHT		CROSS-COUNTRY	ACTUAL INSTRUMENT	SIMULATED INSTRUMENT					
											I certify that the statements made by me on this form are true.
											PILOT'S SIGNATURE

YEAR 20__ DATE	AIRCRAFT MAKE and MODEL	AIRCRAFT IDENTIFCATION NUMBER	POINTS OF DEPARTURE & ARRIVAL		AIRCRAFT CATEGORY and CLASSIFICATION					TYPE OF PILOTING TIME							
			FROM	TO	AIRPLANE SINGLE ENGINE LAND		AIRPLANE MULTI-ENGINE LAND		ROTORCRAFT HELICOPTER				DUAL RECEIVED		PILOT-IN-COMMAND	SECOND-IN-COMMAND	AS FLIGHT INSTRUCTOR
			PAGE TOTAL														
			AMOUNT FORWARD														
			TOTAL TO DATE														

GROUND TRAINER	CONDITIONS OF FLIGHT						NO. INSTR. APPR.	NO. LDG. DAY/NIGHT	TOTAL DURATION OF FLIGHT	REMARKS PROCEDURES, MANEUVERS, ENDORSEMENTS
	DAY		NIGHT		CROSS-COUNTRY	ACTUAL INSTRUMENT	SIMULATED INSTRUMENT				
											I certify that the statements made by me on this form are true.
											PILOT'S SIGNATURE

YEAR 20__ DATE	AIRCRAFT MAKE and MODEL	AIRCRAFT IDENTIFCATION NUMBER	POINTS OF DEPARTURE & ARRIVAL		AIRCRAFT CATEGORY and CLASSIFICATION					TYPE OF PILOTING TIME			
			FROM	TO	AIRPLANE SINGLE ENGINE LAND	AIRPLANE MULTI-ENGINE LAND	ROTORCRAFT HELICOPTER			DUAL RECEIVED	PILOT-IN-COMMAND	SECOND-IN-COMMAND	AS FLIGHT INSTRUCTOR
			PAGE TOTAL										
			AMOUNT FORWARD										
			TOTAL TO DATE										

GROUND TRAINER	CONDITIONS OF FLIGHT						NO. INSTR. APPR.	NO. LDG. DAY/NIGHT	TOTAL DURATION OF FLIGHT		REMARKS PROCEDURES, MANEUVERS, ENDORSEMENTS
	DAY	NIGHT	CROSS-COUNTRY		ACTUAL INSTRUMENT	SIMULATED INSTRUMENT					
											I certify that the statements made by me on this form are true.
											PILOT'S SIGNATURE

YEAR 20___ DATE	AIRCRAFT MAKE and MODEL	AIRCRAFT IDENTIFCATION NUMBER	POINTS OF DEPARTURE & ARRIVAL		AIRCRAFT CATEGORY and CLASSIFICATION				TYPE OF PILOTING TIME			
			FROM	TO	AIRPLANE SINGLE ENGINE LAND	AIRPLANE MULTI-ENGINE LAND	ROTORCRAFT HELICOPTER		DUAL RECEIVED	PILOT-IN-COMMAND	SECOND-IN-COMMAND	AS FLIGHT INSTRUCTOR
				PAGE TOTAL								
				AMOUNT FORWARD								
				TOTAL TO DATE								

GROUND TRAINER	CONDITIONS OF FLIGHT						NO. INSTR. APPR.	NO. LDG. DAY / NIGHT	TOTAL DURATION OF FLIGHT		REMARKS PROCEDURES, MANEUVERS, ENDORSEMENTS
	DAY	NIGHT		CROSS-COUNTRY	ACTUAL INSTRUMENT	SIMULATED INSTRUMENT					
											I certify that the statements made by me on this form are true.
											PILOT'S SIGNATURE

YEAR 20___ DATE	AIRCRAFT MAKE and MODEL	AIRCRAFT IDENTIFCATION NUMBER	POINTS OF DEPARTURE & ARRIVAL		AIRCRAFT CATEGORY and CLASSIFICATION					TYPE OF PILOTING TIME			
			FROM	TO	AIRPLANE SINGLE ENGINE LAND	AIRPLANE MULTI-ENGINE LAND	ROTORCRAFT HELICOPTER			DUAL RECEIVED	PILOT-IN-COMMAND	SECOND-IN-COMMAND	AS FLIGHT INSTRUCTOR
				PAGE TOTAL									
				AMOUNT FORWARD									
				TOTAL TO DATE									

GROUND TRAINER		CONDITIONS OF FLIGHT										NO. INSTR. APPR.	NO. LDG. DAY / NIGHT		TOTAL DURATION OF FLIGHT		REMARKS PROCEDURES, MANEUVERS, ENDORSEMENTS
		DAY		NIGHT		CROSS-COUNTRY		ACTUAL INSTRUMENT		SIMULATED INSTRUMENT							
																	I certify that the statements made by me on this form are true.
																	PILOT'S SIGNATURE

YEAR 20___ DATE	AIRCRAFT MAKE and MODEL	AIRCRAFT IDENTIFCATION NUMBER	POINTS OF DEPARTURE & ARRIVAL		AIRCRAFT CATEGORY and CLASSIFICATION					TYPE OF PILOTING TIME							
			FROM	TO	AIRPLANE SINGLE ENGINE LAND		AIRPLANE MULTI-ENGINE LAND		ROTORCRAFT HELICOPTER				DUAL RECEIVED		PILOT-IN-COMMAND	SECOND-IN-COMMAND	AS FLIGHT INSTRUCTOR
			PAGE TOTAL														
			AMOUNT FORWARD														
			TOTAL TO DATE														

GROUND TRAINER	CONDITIONS OF FLIGHT						NO. INSTR. APPR.	NO. LDG. DAY/NIGHT	TOTAL DURATION OF FLIGHT		REMARKS PROCEDURES, MANEUVERS, ENDORSEMENTS
	DAY		NIGHT		CROSS-COUNTRY		ACTUAL INSTRUMENT		SIMULATED INSTRUMENT		
													I certify that the statements made by me on this form are true.
													PILOT'S SIGNATURE

YEAR 20___ DATE	AIRCRAFT MAKE and MODEL	AIRCRAFT IDENTIFCATION NUMBER	POINTS OF DEPARTURE & ARRIVAL		AIRCRAFT CATEGORY and CLASSIFICATION				TYPE OF PILOTING TIME			
			FROM	TO	AIRPLANE SINGLE ENGINE LAND	AIRPLANE MULTI-ENGINE LAND	ROTORCRAFT HELICOPTER		DUAL RECEIVED	PILOT-IN-COMMAND	SECOND-IN-COMMAND	AS FLIGHT INSTRUCTOR
				PAGE TOTAL								
				AMOUNT FORWARD								
				TOTAL TO DATE								

GROUND TRAINER	CONDITIONS OF FLIGHT						NO. INSTR. APPR.	NO. LDG. DAY/NIGHT	TOTAL DURATION OF FLIGHT		REMARKS PROCEDURES, MANEUVERS, ENDORSEMENTS
	DAY	NIGHT	CROSS-COUNTRY		ACTUAL INSTRUMENT	SIMULATED INSTRUMENT					
											I certify that the statements made by me on this form are true.
											PILOT'S SIGNATURE

YEAR 20___ DATE	AIRCRAFT MAKE and MODEL	AIRCRAFT IDENTIFCATION NUMBER	POINTS OF DEPARTURE & ARRIVAL		AIRCRAFT CATEGORY and CLASSIFICATION					TYPE OF PILOTING TIME			
			FROM	TO	AIRPLANE SINGLE ENGINE LAND	AIRPLANE MULTI-ENGINE LAND	ROTORCRAFT HELICOPTER			DUAL RECEIVED	PILOT-IN-COMMAND	SECOND-IN-COMMAND	AS FLIGHT INSTRUCTOR
			PAGE TOTAL										
			AMOUNT FORWARD										
			TOTAL TO DATE										

GROUND TRAINER	CONDITIONS OF FLIGHT						NO. INSTR. APPR.	NO. LDG. DAY/NIGHT	TOTAL DURATION OF FLIGHT		REMARKS PROCEDURES, MANEUVERS, ENDORSEMENTS
	DAY	NIGHT		CROSS-COUNTRY	ACTUAL INSTRUMENT	SIMULATED INSTRUMENT					
											I certify that the statements made by me on this form are true.
											PILOT'S SIGNATURE

YEAR 20___ DATE	AIRCRAFT MAKE and MODEL	AIRCRAFT IDENTIFCATION NUMBER	POINTS OF DEPARTURE & ARRIVAL		AIRCRAFT CATEGORY and CLASSIFICATION						TYPE OF PILOTING TIME							
			FROM	TO	AIRPLANE SINGLE ENGINE LAND		AIRPLANE MULTI-ENGINE LAND		ROTORCRAFT HELICOPTER		DUAL RECEIVED		PILOT-IN-COMMAND		SECOND-IN-COMMAND		AS FLIGHT INSTRUCTOR
				PAGE TOTAL													
				AMOUNT FORWARD													
				TOTAL TO DATE													

GROUND TRAINER	CONDITIONS OF FLIGHT					NO. INSTR. APPR.	NO. LDG. DAY/NIGHT	TOTAL DURATION OF FLIGHT	REMARKS PROCEDURES, MANEUVERS, ENDORSEMENTS
	DAY	NIGHT	CROSS-COUNTRY	ACTUAL INSTRUMENT	SIMULATED INSTRUMENT				
									I certify that the statements made by me on this form are true.
									PILOT'S SIGNATURE

YEAR 20__ DATE	AIRCRAFT MAKE and MODEL	AIRCRAFT IDENTIFCATION NUMBER	POINTS OF DEPARTURE & ARRIVAL		AIRCRAFT CATEGORY and CLASSIFICATION					TYPE OF PILOTING TIME			
			FROM	TO	AIRPLANE SINGLE ENGINE LAND	AIRPLANE MULTI-ENGINE LAND	ROTORCRAFT HELICOPTER			DUAL RECEIVED	PILOT-IN-COMMAND	SECOND-IN-COMMAND	AS FLIGHT INSTRUCTOR
			PAGE TOTAL										
			AMOUNT FORWARD										
			TOTAL TO DATE										

GROUND TRAINER	CONDITIONS OF FLIGHT						NO. INSTR. APPR.	NO. LDG. DAY / NIGHT		TOTAL DURATION OF FLIGHT	REMARKS PROCEDURES, MANEUVERS, ENDORSEMENTS
	DAY		NIGHT		CROSS-COUNTRY		ACTUAL INSTRUMENT		SIMULATED INSTRUMENT		
													I certify that the statements made by me on this form are true.
													PILOT'S SIGNATURE

YEAR 20___ DATE	AIRCRAFT MAKE and MODEL	AIRCRAFT IDENTIFCATION NUMBER	POINTS OF DEPARTURE & ARRIVAL		AIRCRAFT CATEGORY and CLASSIFICATION								TYPE OF PILOTING TIME							
			FROM	TO	AIRPLANE SINGLE ENGINE LAND		AIRPLANE MULTI-ENGINE LAND		ROTORCRAFT HELICOPTER				DUAL RECEIVED		PILOT-IN-COMMAND		SECOND-IN-COMMAND		AS FLIGHT INSTRUCTOR	
			PAGE TOTAL																	
			AMOUNT FORWARD																	
			TOTAL TO DATE																	

GROUND TRAINER	CONDITIONS OF FLIGHT						NO. INSTR. APPR.	NO. LDG. DAY/NIGHT	TOTAL DURATION OF FLIGHT		REMARKS PROCEDURES, MANEUVERS, ENDORSEMENTS
	DAY		NIGHT		CROSS-COUNTRY	ACTUAL INSTRUMENT	SIMULATED INSTRUMENT				
											I certify that the statements made by me on this form are true.
											PILOT'S SIGNATURE

YEAR 20___ DATE	AIRCRAFT MAKE and MODEL	AIRCRAFT IDENTIFCATION NUMBER	POINTS OF DEPARTURE & ARRIVAL		AIRCRAFT CATEGORY and CLASSIFICATION					TYPE OF PILOTING TIME							
			FROM	TO	AIRPLANE SINGLE ENGINE LAND	AIRPLANE MULTI-ENGINE LAND	ROTORCRAFT HELICOPTER			DUAL RECEIVED		PILOT-IN-COMMAND		SECOND-IN-COMMAND		AS FLIGHT INSTRUCTOR	
			PAGE TOTAL														
			AMOUNT FORWARD														
			TOTAL TO DATE														

GROUND TRAINER	CONDITIONS OF FLIGHT						NO. INSTR. APPR.	NO. LDG. DAY/NIGHT	TOTAL DURATION OF FLIGHT		REMARKS PROCEDURES, MANEUVERS, ENDORSEMENTS
	DAY		NIGHT		CROSS-COUNTRY		ACTUAL INSTRUMENT	SIMULATED INSTRUMENT			
											I certify that the statements made by me on this form are true.
											PILOT'S SIGNATURE

YEAR 20___ DATE	AIRCRAFT MAKE and MODEL	AIRCRAFT IDENTIFCATION NUMBER	POINTS OF DEPARTURE & ARRIVAL		AIRCRAFT CATEGORY and CLASSIFICATION					TYPE OF PILOTING TIME							
			FROM	TO	AIRPLANE SINGLE ENGINE LAND	AIRPLANE MULTI-ENGINE LAND	ROTORCRAFT HELICOPTER			DUAL RECEIVED		PILOT-IN-COMMAND		SECOND-IN-COMMAND		AS FLIGHT INSTRUCTOR	
				PAGE TOTAL													
				AMOUNT FORWARD													
				TOTAL TO DATE													

GROUND TRAINER	CONDITIONS OF FLIGHT						NO. INSTR. APPR.	NO. LDG. DAY/NIGHT	TOTAL DURATION OF FLIGHT	REMARKS PROCEDURES, MANEUVERS, ENDORSEMENTS
	DAY	NIGHT		CROSS-COUNTRY	ACTUAL INSTRUMENT	SIMULATED INSTRUMENT				
										I certify that the statements made by me on this form are true.
										PILOT'S SIGNATURE

YEAR 20___ DATE	AIRCRAFT MAKE and MODEL	AIRCRAFT IDENTIFCATION NUMBER	POINTS OF DEPARTURE & ARRIVAL		AIRCRAFT CATEGORY and CLASSIFICATION					TYPE OF PILOTING TIME			
			FROM	TO	AIRPLANE SINGLE ENGINE LAND	AIRPLANE MULTI-ENGINE LAND	ROTORCRAFT HELICOPTER			DUAL RECEIVED	PILOT-IN-COMMAND	SECOND-IN-COMMAND	AS FLIGHT INSTRUCTOR
			PAGE TOTAL										
			AMOUNT FORWARD										
			TOTAL TO DATE										

GROUND TRAINER	CONDITIONS OF FLIGHT						NO. INSTR. APPR.	NO. LDG. DAY/NIGHT	TOTAL DURATION OF FLIGHT		REMARKS – PROCEDURES, MANEUVERS, ENDORSEMENTS
	DAY		NIGHT		CROSS-COUNTRY	ACTUAL INSTRUMENT	SIMULATED INSTRUMENT					

I certify that the statements made by me on this form are true.

_____
PILOT'S SIGNATURE

YEAR 20___ DATE	AIRCRAFT MAKE and MODEL	AIRCRAFT IDENTIFCATION NUMBER	POINTS OF DEPARTURE & ARRIVAL		AIRCRAFT CATEGORY and CLASSIFICATION					TYPE OF PILOTING TIME			
			FROM	TO	AIRPLANE SINGLE ENGINE LAND	AIRPLANE MULTI-ENGINE LAND	ROTORCRAFT HELICOPTER			DUAL RECEIVED	PILOT-IN-COMMAND	SECOND-IN-COMMAND	AS FLIGHT INSTRUCTOR
				PAGE TOTAL									
				AMOUNT FORWARD									
				TOTAL TO DATE									

GROUND TRAINER	CONDITIONS OF FLIGHT						NO. INSTR. APPR.	NO. LDG. DAY / NIGHT	TOTAL DURATION OF FLIGHT		REMARKS PROCEDURES, MANEUVERS, ENDORSEMENTS
	DAY		NIGHT		CROSS-COUNTRY		ACTUAL INSTRUMENT	SIMULATED INSTRUMENT			
											I certify that the statements made by me on this form are true.
											PILOT'S SIGNATURE

YEAR 20__ DATE	AIRCRAFT MAKE and MODEL	AIRCRAFT IDENTIFCATION NUMBER	POINTS OF DEPARTURE & ARRIVAL		AIRCRAFT CATEGORY and CLASSIFICATION						TYPE OF PILOTING TIME							
			FROM	TO	AIRPLANE SINGLE ENGINE LAND		AIRPLANE MULTI-ENGINE LAND		ROTORCRAFT HELICOPTER				DUAL RECEIVED		PILOT-IN-COMMAND		SECOND-IN-COMMAND		AS FLIGHT INSTRUCTOR
			PAGE TOTAL																
			AMOUNT FORWARD																
			TOTAL TO DATE																

GROUND TRAINER	CONDITIONS OF FLIGHT						NO. INSTR. APPR.	NO. LDG. DAY/NIGHT	TOTAL DURATION OF FLIGHT		REMARKS PROCEDURES, MANEUVERS, ENDORSEMENTS
	DAY		NIGHT		CROSS-COUNTRY		ACTUAL INSTRUMENT	SIMULATED INSTRUMENT			
											I certify that the statements made by me on this form are true.
											PILOT'S SIGNATURE

YEAR 20___ DATE	AIRCRAFT MAKE and MODEL	AIRCRAFT IDENTIFCATION NUMBER	POINTS OF DEPARTURE & ARRIVAL		AIRCRAFT CATEGORY and CLASSIFICATION					TYPE OF PILOTING TIME			
			FROM	TO	AIRPLANE SINGLE ENGINE LAND	AIRPLANE MULTI-ENGINE LAND	ROTORCRAFT HELICOPTER			DUAL RECEIVED	PILOT-IN-COMMAND	SECOND-IN-COMMAND	AS FLIGHT INSTRUCTOR
			PAGE TOTAL										
			AMOUNT FORWARD										
			TOTAL TO DATE										

GROUND TRAINER	CONDITIONS OF FLIGHT						NO. INSTR. APPR.	NO. LDG. DAY/NIGHT	TOTAL DURATION OF FLIGHT	REMARKS PROCEDURES, MANEUVERS, ENDORSEMENTS
	DAY	NIGHT	CROSS-COUNTRY	ACTUAL INSTRUMENT	SIMULATED INSTRUMENT					
										I certify that the statements made by me on this form are true.
										PILOT'S SIGNATURE

YEAR 20___ DATE	AIRCRAFT MAKE and MODEL	AIRCRAFT IDENTIFCATION NUMBER	POINTS OF DEPARTURE & ARRIVAL		AIRCRAFT CATEGORY and CLASSIFICATION					TYPE OF PILOTING TIME								
			FROM	TO	AIRPLANE SINGLE ENGINE LAND		AIRPLANE MULTI-ENGINE LAND		ROTORCRAFT HELICOPTER				DUAL RECEIVED		PILOT-IN-COMMAND		SECOND-IN-COMMAND		AS FLIGHT INSTRUCTOR	
				PAGE TOTAL																
				AMOUNT FORWARD																
				TOTAL TO DATE																

GROUND TRAINER	CONDITIONS OF FLIGHT									NO. INSTR. APPR.	NO. LDG. DAY/NIGHT		TOTAL DURATION OF FLIGHT		REMARKS PROCEDURES, MANEUVERS, ENDORSEMENTS
	DAY		NIGHT		CROSS-COUNTRY		ACTUAL INSTRUMENT		SIMULATED INSTRUMENT						
															I certify that the statements made by me on this form are true.
															PILOT'S SIGNATURE

YEAR 20___ DATE	AIRCRAFT MAKE and MODEL	AIRCRAFT IDENTIFCATION NUMBER	POINTS OF DEPARTURE & ARRIVAL		AIRCRAFT CATEGORY and CLASSIFICATION					TYPE OF PILOTING TIME							
			FROM	TO	AIRPLANE SINGLE ENGINE LAND		AIRPLANE MULTI-ENGINE LAND		ROTORCRAFT HELICOPTER			DUAL RECEIVED		PILOT-IN-COMMAND		SECOND-IN-COMMAND		AS FLIGHT INSTRUCTOR
			PAGE TOTAL															
			AMOUNT FORWARD															
			TOTAL TO DATE															

GROUND TRAINER	CONDITIONS OF FLIGHT						NO. INSTR. APPR.	NO. LDG. DAY/NIGHT	TOTAL DURATION OF FLIGHT	REMARKS PROCEDURES, MANEUVERS, ENDORSEMENTS
	DAY	NIGHT	CROSS-COUNTRY	ACTUAL INSTRUMENT	SIMULATED INSTRUMENT					
									I certify that the statements made by me on this form are true.
										PILOT'S SIGNATURE

YEAR 20___ DATE	AIRCRAFT MAKE and MODEL	AIRCRAFT IDENTIFCATION NUMBER	POINTS OF DEPARTURE & ARRIVAL		AIRCRAFT CATEGORY and CLASSIFICATION						TYPE OF PILOTING TIME			
			FROM	TO	AIRPLANE SINGLE ENGINE LAND		AIRPLANE MULTI-ENGINE LAND		ROTORCRAFT HELICOPTER		DUAL RECEIVED	PILOT-IN-COMMAND	SECOND-IN-COMMAND	AS FLIGHT INSTRUCTOR
				PAGE TOTAL										
				AMOUNT FORWARD										
				TOTAL TO DATE										

GROUND TRAINER	CONDITIONS OF FLIGHT						NO. INSTR. APPR.	NO. LDG.		TOTAL DURATION OF FLIGHT		REMARKS PROCEDURES, MANEUVERS, ENDORSEMENTS
	DAY		NIGHT		CROSS-COUNTRY	ACTUAL INSTRUMENT	SIMULATED INSTRUMENT		DAY	NIGHT		
											I certify that the statements made by me on this form are true.
												PILOT'S SIGNATURE

YEAR 20__ DATE	AIRCRAFT MAKE and MODEL	AIRCRAFT IDENTIFCATION NUMBER	POINTS OF DEPARTURE & ARRIVAL		AIRCRAFT CATEGORY and CLASSIFICATION					TYPE OF PILOTING TIME						
			FROM	TO	AIRPLANE SINGLE ENGINE LAND		AIRPLANE MULTI-ENGINE LAND		ROTORCRAFT HELICOPTER			DUAL RECEIVED		PILOT-IN-COMMAND	SECOND-IN-COMMAND	AS FLIGHT INSTRUCTOR
			PAGE TOTAL													
			AMOUNT FORWARD													
			TOTAL TO DATE													

GROUND TRAINER	CONDITIONS OF FLIGHT						NO. INSTR. APPR.	NO. LDG. DAY/NIGHT	TOTAL DURATION OF FLIGHT		REMARKS PROCEDURES, MANEUVERS, ENDORSEMENTS
	DAY		NIGHT		CROSS-COUNTRY		ACTUAL INSTRUMENT	SIMULATED INSTRUMENT			
											I certify that the statements made by me on this form are true.
											PILOT'S SIGNATURE

YEAR 20___ DATE	AIRCRAFT MAKE and MODEL	AIRCRAFT IDENTIFCATION NUMBER	POINTS OF DEPARTURE & ARRIVAL		AIRCRAFT CATEGORY and CLASSIFICATION								TYPE OF PILOTING TIME							
			FROM	TO	AIRPLANE SINGLE ENGINE LAND		AIRPLANE MULTI-ENGINE LAND		ROTORCRAFT HELICOPTER				DUAL RECEIVED		PILOT-IN-COMMAND		SECOND-IN-COMMAND		AS FLIGHT INSTRUCTOR	
			PAGE TOTAL																	
			AMOUNT FORWARD																	
			TOTAL TO DATE																	

GROUND TRAINER	CONDITIONS OF FLIGHT						NO. INSTR. APPR.	NO. LDG. DAY/NIGHT	TOTAL DURATION OF FLIGHT	REMARKS PROCEDURES, MANEUVERS, ENDORSEMENTS
	DAY	NIGHT	CROSS-COUNTRY	ACTUAL INSTRUMENT	SIMULATED INSTRUMENT					
										I certify that the statements made by me on this form are true.
										PILOT'S SIGNATURE

YEAR 20___ DATE	AIRCRAFT MAKE and MODEL	AIRCRAFT IDENTIFCATION NUMBER	POINTS OF DEPARTURE & ARRIVAL		AIRCRAFT CATEGORY and CLASSIFICATION					TYPE OF PILOTING TIME							
			FROM	TO	AIRPLANE SINGLE ENGINE LAND		AIRPLANE MULTI-ENGINE LAND		ROTORCRAFT HELICOPTER				DUAL RECEIVED		PILOT-IN-COMMAND	SECOND-IN-COMMAND	AS FLIGHT INSTRUCTOR
				PAGE TOTAL													
				AMOUNT FORWARD													
				TOTAL TO DATE													

GROUND TRAINER	CONDITIONS OF FLIGHT											NO. INSTR. APPR.	NO. LDG. DAY/NIGHT	TOTAL DURATION OF FLIGHT		REMARKS PROCEDURES, MANEUVERS, ENDORSEMENTS
	DAY		NIGHT		CROSS-COUNTRY		ACTUAL INSTRUMENT		SIMULATED INSTRUMENT						

I certify that the statements made by me on this form are true.

_____

PILOT'S SIGNATURE

YEAR 20___ DATE	AIRCRAFT MAKE and MODEL	AIRCRAFT IDENTIFCATION NUMBER	POINTS OF DEPARTURE & ARRIVAL		AIRCRAFT CATEGORY and CLASSIFICATION					TYPE OF PILOTING TIME				
			FROM	TO	AIRPLANE SINGLE ENGINE LAND	AIRPLANE MULTI-ENGINE LAND	ROTORCRAFT HELICOPTER			DUAL RECEIVED	PILOT-IN-COMMAND	SECOND-IN-COMMAND		AS FLIGHT INSTRUCTOR
				PAGE TOTAL										
				AMOUNT FORWARD										
				TOTAL TO DATE										

GROUND TRAINER	CONDITIONS OF FLIGHT								NO. INSTR. APPR.	NO. LDG. DAY/NIGHT		TOTAL DURATION OF FLIGHT		REMARKS PROCEDURES, MANEUVERS, ENDORSEMENTS
	DAY		NIGHT		CROSS-COUNTRY		ACTUAL INSTRUMENT	SIMULATED INSTRUMENT						
														I certify that the statements made by me on this form are true.
														PILOT'S SIGNATURE

YEAR 20___ DATE	AIRCRAFT MAKE and MODEL	AIRCRAFT IDENTIFCATION NUMBER	POINTS OF DEPARTURE & ARRIVAL		AIRCRAFT CATEGORY and CLASSIFICATION					TYPE OF PILOTING TIME			
			FROM	TO	AIRPLANE SINGLE ENGINE LAND	AIRPLANE MULTI-ENGINE LAND	ROTORCRAFT HELICOPTER			DUAL RECEIVED	PILOT-IN-COMMAND	SECOND-IN-COMMAND	AS FLIGHT INSTRUCTOR
				PAGE TOTAL									
				AMOUNT FORWARD									
				TOTAL TO DATE									

GROUND TRAINER	CONDITIONS OF FLIGHT											NO. INSTR. APPR.	NO. LDG. DAY/NIGHT		TOTAL DURATION OF FLIGHT		REMARKS PROCEDURES, MANEUVERS, ENDORSEMENTS
	DAY		NIGHT		CROSS-COUNTRY		ACTUAL INSTRUMENT		SIMULATED INSTRUMENT								
																	I certify that the statements made by me on this form are true.
																	PILOT'S SIGNATURE

YEAR 20___ DATE	AIRCRAFT MAKE and MODEL	AIRCRAFT IDENTIFCATION NUMBER	POINTS OF DEPARTURE & ARRIVAL		AIRCRAFT CATEGORY and CLASSIFICATION					TYPE OF PILOTING TIME							
			FROM	TO	AIRPLANE SINGLE ENGINE LAND		AIRPLANE MULTI-ENGINE LAND		ROTORCRAFT HELICOPTER				DUAL RECEIVED		PILOT-IN-COMMAND	SECOND-IN-COMMAND	AS FLIGHT INSTRUCTOR
				PAGE TOTAL													
				AMOUNT FORWARD													
				TOTAL TO DATE													

GROUND TRAINER	CONDITIONS OF FLIGHT						NO. INSTR. APPR.	NO. LDG. DAY/NIGHT	TOTAL DURATION OF FLIGHT		REMARKS PROCEDURES, MANEUVERS, ENDORSEMENTS
	DAY		NIGHT		CROSS-COUNTRY		ACTUAL INSTRUMENT		SIMULATED INSTRUMENT		
											I certify that the statements made by me on this form are true.
											PILOT'S SIGNATURE

YEAR 20___ DATE	AIRCRAFT MAKE and MODEL	AIRCRAFT IDENTIFCATION NUMBER	POINTS OF DEPARTURE & ARRIVAL		AIRCRAFT CATEGORY and CLASSIFICATION					TYPE OF PILOTING TIME							
			FROM	TO	AIRPLANE SINGLE ENGINE LAND	AIRPLANE MULTI-ENGINE LAND	ROTORCRAFT HELICOPTER			DUAL RECEIVED		PILOT-IN-COMMAND		SECOND-IN-COMMAND		AS FLIGHT INSTRUCTOR	
				PAGE TOTAL													
				AMOUNT FORWARD													
				TOTAL TO DATE													

GROUND TRAINER	CONDITIONS OF FLIGHT						NO. INSTR. APPR.	NO. LDG. DAY/NIGHT	TOTAL DURATION OF FLIGHT	REMARKS PROCEDURES, MANEUVERS, ENDORSEMENTS
	DAY		NIGHT		CROSS-COUNTRY		ACTUAL INSTRUMENT		SIMULATED INSTRUMENT	
										I certify that the statements made by me on this form are true.
										PILOT'S SIGNATURE

YEAR 20___ DATE	AIRCRAFT MAKE and MODEL	AIRCRAFT IDENTIFCATION NUMBER	POINTS OF DEPARTURE & ARRIVAL		AIRCRAFT CATEGORY and CLASSIFICATION					TYPE OF PILOTING TIME							
			FROM	TO	AIRPLANE SINGLE ENGINE LAND		AIRPLANE MULTI-ENGINE LAND		ROTORCRAFT HELICOPTER			DUAL RECEIVED		PILOT-IN-COMMAND		SECOND-IN-COMMAND		AS FLIGHT INSTRUCTOR	
				PAGE TOTAL															
				AMOUNT FORWARD															
				TOTAL TO DATE															

GROUND TRAINER	CONDITIONS OF FLIGHT											NO. INSTR. APPR.	NO. LDG. DAY/NIGHT	TOTAL DURATION OF FLIGHT		REMARKS PROCEDURES, MANEUVERS, ENDORSEMENTS
	DAY		NIGHT		CROSS-COUNTRY		ACTUAL INSTRUMENT		SIMULATED INSTRUMENT						
																I certify that the statements made by me on this form are true.
																PILOT'S SIGNATURE

YEAR 20__ DATE	AIRCRAFT MAKE and MODEL	AIRCRAFT IDENTIFCATION NUMBER	POINTS OF DEPARTURE & ARRIVAL		AIRCRAFT CATEGORY and CLASSIFICATION				TYPE OF PILOTING TIME			
			FROM	TO	AIRPLANE SINGLE ENGINE LAND	AIRPLANE MULTI-ENGINE LAND	ROTORCRAFT HELICOPTER		DUAL RECEIVED	PILOT-IN-COMMAND	SECOND-IN-COMMAND	AS FLIGHT INSTRUCTOR
			PAGE TOTAL									
			AMOUNT FORWARD									
			TOTAL TO DATE									

GROUND TRAINER		CONDITIONS OF FLIGHT										NO. INSTR. APPR.	NO. LDG. DAY / NIGHT		TOTAL DURATION OF FLIGHT		REMARKS PROCEDURES, MANEUVERS, ENDORSEMENTS
		DAY		NIGHT		CROSS-COUNTRY		ACTUAL INSTRUMENT		SIMULATED INSTRUMENT							
																	I certify that the statements made by me on this form are true.
																	PILOT'S SIGNATURE

YEAR 20__ DATE	AIRCRAFT MAKE and MODEL	AIRCRAFT IDENTIFCATION NUMBER	POINTS OF DEPARTURE & ARRIVAL		AIRCRAFT CATEGORY and CLASSIFICATION					TYPE OF PILOTING TIME								
			FROM	TO	AIRPLANE SINGLE ENGINE LAND		AIRPLANE MULTI-ENGINE LAND		ROTORCRAFT HELICOPTER				DUAL RECEIVED		PILOT-IN-COMMAND		SECOND-IN-COMMAND		AS FLIGHT INSTRUCTOR	
			PAGE TOTAL																	
			AMOUNT FORWARD																	
			TOTAL TO DATE																	

GROUND TRAINER	CONDITIONS OF FLIGHT						NO. INSTR. APPR.	NO. LDG. DAY/NIGHT	TOTAL DURATION OF FLIGHT	REMARKS PROCEDURES, MANEUVERS, ENDORSEMENTS
	DAY		NIGHT		CROSS-COUNTRY		ACTUAL INSTRUMENT	SIMULATED INSTRUMENT		
											I certify that the statements made by me on this form are true.
											PILOT'S SIGNATURE

YEAR 20___ DATE	AIRCRAFT MAKE and MODEL	AIRCRAFT IDENTIFCATION NUMBER	POINTS OF DEPARTURE & ARRIVAL		AIRCRAFT CATEGORY and CLASSIFICATION				TYPE OF PILOTING TIME			
			FROM	TO	AIRPLANE SINGLE ENGINE LAND	AIRPLANE MULTI-ENGINE LAND	ROTORCRAFT HELICOPTER		DUAL RECEIVED	PILOT-IN-COMMAND	SECOND-IN-COMMAND	AS FLIGHT INSTRUCTOR
				PAGE TOTAL								
				AMOUNT FORWARD								
				TOTAL TO DATE								

GROUND TRAINER		CONDITIONS OF FLIGHT							NO. INSTR. APPR.	NO. LDG. DAY/NIGHT		TOTAL DURATION OF FLIGHT		REMARKS PROCEDURES, MANEUVERS, ENDORSEMENTS
		DAY		NIGHT		CROSS-COUNTRY		ACTUAL INSTRUMENT		SIMULATED INSTRUMENT				
														I certify that the statements made by me on this form are true.
														PILOT'S SIGNATURE

CLASSIFICATION OF PILOT-IN-COMMAND TIME

YEAR: _____	JAN	FEB	MAR	APR	MAY	JUNE	JULY	AUG	SEP	OCT	NOV	DEC	**TOTAL LAST 12 MONTHS**
SINGLE ENGINE													
SINGLE ENGINE OVER 12,500 POUNDS													
TWIN ENGINE													
FOUR ENGINE													
MULTI-ENGINE OVER 12,500 POUNDS													
EXECUTIVE TRANSPORT													
TURBOJET													
TURBO-PROP													
HELICOPTER													
GYROPLANE													
GLIDER													
POWERED PARACHUTE													
WEIGHT-SHIFT CONTROL													
ACTUAL INSTRUMENT													
SIMULATED INSTRUMENT													
GROUND TRAINER													
NIGHT													
CROSS-COUNTRY													
PRIMARY INSTRUCTOR													
ADVANCED INSTRUCTOR													
INSTRUMENT INSTRUCTOR													
MULTI-ENGINE INSTRUCTOR													
HELICOPTER INSTRUCTOR													
SCHEDULED AIR CARRIER													
AERIAL APPLICATION													
PRESSURIZED AIRCRAFT													

CLASSIFICATION OF PILOT-IN-COMMAND TIME

YEAR: _____	JAN	FEB	MAR	APR	MAY	JUNE	JULY	AUG	SEP	OCT	NOV	DEC	TOTAL LAST 12 MONTHS
SINGLE ENGINE													
SINGLE ENGINE OVER 12,500 POUNDS													
TWIN ENGINE													
FOUR ENGINE													
MULTI-ENGINE OVER 12,500 POUNDS													
EXECUTIVE TRANSPORT													
TURBOJET													
TURBO-PROP													
HELICOPTER													
GYROPLANE													
GLIDER													
POWERED PARACHUTE													
WEIGHT-SHIFT CONTROL													
ACTUAL INSTRUMENT													
SIMULATED INSTRUMENT													
GROUND TRAINER													
NIGHT													
CROSS-COUNTRY													
PRIMARY INSTRUCTOR													
ADVANCED INSTRUCTOR													
INSTRUMENT INSTRUCTOR													
MULTI-ENGINE INSTRUCTOR													
HELICOPTER INSTRUCTOR													
SCHEDULED AIR CARRIER													
AERIAL APPLICATION													
PRESSURIZED AIRCRAFT													

CLASSIFICATION OF PILOT-IN-COMMAND TIME

YEAR: _____	JAN	FEB	MAR	APR	MAY	JUNE	JULY	AUG	SEP	OCT	NOV	DEC	TOTAL LAST 12 MONTHS
SINGLE ENGINE													
SINGLE ENGINE OVER 12,500 POUNDS													
TWIN ENGINE													
FOUR ENGINE													
MULTI-ENGINE OVER 12,500 POUNDS													
EXECUTIVE TRANSPORT													
TURBOJET													
TURBO-PROP													
HELICOPTER													
GYROPLANE													
GLIDER													
POWERED PARACHUTE													
WEIGHT-SHIFT CONTROL													
ACTUAL INSTRUMENT													
SIMULATED INSTRUMENT													
GROUND TRAINER													
NIGHT													
CROSS-COUNTRY													
PRIMARY INSTRUCTOR													
ADVANCED INSTRUCTOR													
INSTRUMENT INSTRUCTOR													
MULTI-ENGINE INSTRUCTOR													
HELICOPTER INSTRUCTOR													
SCHEDULED AIR CARRIER													
AERIAL APPLICATION													
PRESSURIZED AIRCRAFT													

CLASSIFICATION OF PILOT-IN-COMMAND TIME

YEAR: _____	JAN	FEB	MAR	APR	MAY	JUNE	JULY	AUG	SEP	OCT	NOV	DEC	TOTAL LAST 12 MONTHS
SINGLE ENGINE													
SINGLE ENGINE OVER 12,500 POUNDS													
TWIN ENGINE													
FOUR ENGINE													
MULTI-ENGINE OVER 12,500 POUNDS													
EXECUTIVE TRANSPORT													
TURBOJET													
TURBO-PROP													
HELICOPTER													
GYROPLANE													
GLIDER													
POWERED PARACHUTE													
WEIGHT-SHIFT CONTROL													
ACTUAL INSTRUMENT													
SIMULATED INSTRUMENT													
GROUND TRAINER													
NIGHT													
CROSS-COUNTRY													
PRIMARY INSTRUCTOR													
ADVANCED INSTRUCTOR													
INSTRUMENT INSTRUCTOR													
MULTI-ENGINE INSTRUCTOR													
HELICOPTER INSTRUCTOR													
SCHEDULED AIR CARRIER													
AERIAL APPLICATION													
PRESSURIZED AIRCRAFT													

AIRCRAFT FLOWN and NUMBER OF HOURS IN EACH AS PILOT-IN-COMMAND and _____

AIRCRAFT MAKE and MODEL	PIC		AIRCRAFT MAKE and MODEL	PIC		AIRCRAFT MAKE and MODEL	PIC	

INITIAL SOLO ENDORSEMENTS

I certify that *(First name, MI, Last name)* _____, has satisfactorily completed the presolo knowledge exam of §61.87(b), received the required presolo training required by §61.87(c), and has demonstrated the proficiency of §61.87(d) and is proficient to make solo flights in *(make and model aircraft)* _____.
SIGNED _____ DATE _____
CFI NO. _____ EXPIRATION DATE _____

I certify that *(First name, MI, Last name)* _____, has received the required training to qualify for local solo flying. I have determined he/she meets the applicable requirements of §61.87(n) and is proficient to make solo flights in *(make and model aircraft)* _____ until *(maximum 90 days from date given)* _____.
Limitations: _____.
SIGNED _____ DATE _____
CFI NO. _____ EXPIRATION DATE _____

ADDITIONAL AIRPORT WITHIN 25NM SOLO ENDORSEMENTS

I certify that *(First name, MI, Last name)* _____, has received the required training of § 61.93(b)(1). I have determined that he/she is proficient to practice solo takeoffs and landings at *(airport name)* _____ subject to the following conditions: _____.
SIGNED _____ DATE _____
CFI NO. _____ EXPIRATION DATE _____

I certify that *(First name, MI, Last name)* _____, has received the required training of § 61.93(b)(1). I have determined that he/she is proficient to practice solo takeoffs and landings at *(airport name)* _____ subject to the following conditions: _____.
SIGNED _____ DATE _____
CFI NO. _____ EXPIRATION DATE _____

CROSS-COUNTRY SOLO ENDORSEMENTS

I certify that *(First name, MI, Last name)* _____, has received the required solo cross-country training and find he/she has met the applicable requirements of §61.93, and is proficient to make solo cross-country flights in a *(make and model aircraft)* _____.
SIGNED _____ DATE _____
CFI NO. _____ EXPIRATION DATE _____

I have reviewed the cross-country planning of *(First name, MI, Last name)* _____ and find the planning and preparation to be correct to make the solo flight from *(location)* _____ to *(destination)* _____ via *(route of flight)* _____ with landings at *(name the airports)* _____ in a *(make and model aircraft)* _____ on *(date)* _____.
List any applicable conditions or limitations: _____
SIGNED _____ DATE _____
CFI NO. _____ EXPIRATION DATE _____

ADDITIONAL SOLO ENDORSEMENTS

90-DAY SOLO

I certify that *(First name, MI, Last name)* _____,
has received the required training to qualify for local solo flying. I have determined he/she meets the applicable requirements of §61.87(n) and is proficient to make solo flights in *(make and model aircraft)* _____
until *(maximum 90 days from date given)* _____.
Limitations: _____.
SIGNED _____ DATE _____
CFI NO. _____ EXPIRATION DATE _____

CLASS B SOLO

I certify that *(First name, MI, Last name)* _____,
has received the required training of §61.95(a) and determined he/she is proficient to conduct solo flights in *(name of Class B)* _____
airspace. *List any applicable conditions or limitations:* _____
_____.
SIGNED _____ DATE _____
CFI NO. _____ EXPIRATION DATE _____

I certify that *(First name, MI, Last name)* _____,
has received the required training to qualify for local solo flying. I have determined he/she meets the applicable requirements of §61.87(n) and is proficient to make solo flights in *(make and model aircraft)* _____
until *(maximum 90 days from date given)* _____.
Limitations: _____.
SIGNED _____ DATE _____
CFI NO. _____ EXPIRATION DATE _____

I certify that *(First name, MI, Last name)* _____,
has received the required training of §61.95(a)(1) and determined that he/she is proficient to conduct solo flight operations at *(name of airport)* _____
_____. *List any applicable conditions or limitations:*
_____.
SIGNED _____ DATE _____
CFI NO. _____ EXPIRATION DATE _____

NIGHT SOLO

I certify that *(First name, MI, Last name)* _____,
has received the required presolo training in a *(make and model aircraft)* _____
_____ and determined he/she has demonstrated the proficiency of §61.87(o) and is proficient to make solo flights at night in a *(make and model aircraft)* _____
SIGNED _____ DATE _____
CFI NO. _____ EXPIRATION DATE _____

REPEAT X/C SOLO (LESS THAN 50 NM)

I certify that *(First name, MI, Last name)* _____,
has received the required training in both directions between and at both *(airport names)* _____ and determined that he/she is proficient in §61.93(b)(2) to conduct repeated solo cross-country flights over that route, which is not more than 50NM from the point of departure, subject to the following conditions: _____,
SIGNED _____ DATE _____
CFI NO. _____ EXPIRATION DATE _____

INITIAL SPORT PILOT ENDORSEMENTS

SOLO FLIGHT 1st 90-DAY

I certify that *(First name, MI, Last name)* _____,
has received the required training to qualify for local solo flying. I have determined he/she meets the applicable requirements of §61.87(n) and is proficient to make solo flights in *(make and model aircraft)* _____
until *(maximum 90 days from date given)* _____.
Limitations: _____.
SIGNED _____ DATE _____
CFI NO. _____ EXPIRATION DATE _____

SOLO FLIGHT IN CLASS B, C, AND D AIRSPACE *(required each additional 90-day period)*

I certify that *(First name, MI, Last name)* _____,
has received the required training of §61.94(a). I have determined he/she is proficient to conduct solo flights in *(name of Class B, C, or D)* _____ airspace.
List any applicable conditions or limitations: _____.
SIGNED _____ DATE _____
CFI NO. _____ EXPIRATION DATE _____

TAKING THE AERONAUTICAL KNOWLEDGE TEST

I certify that *(First name, MI, Last name)* _____,
has received the required aeronautical knowledge training of §61.309. I have determined that he/she is prepared for the *(name the knowledge test/aircraft category)* _____
SIGNED _____ DATE _____
CFI NO. _____ EXPIRATION DATE _____

TAKING THE SPORT PILOT PRACTICAL TEST

I certify that *(First name, MI, Last name)* _____,
has received the required training of §§61.309 and 61.311 and met the experience requirements of §61.313. I have determined that he/she is prepared for the *(category/class)* _____ practical test.
SIGNED _____ DATE _____
CFI NO. _____ EXPIRATION DATE _____

I certify that *(First name, MI, Last name)* _____,
has received the required training and demonstrated satisfactory knowledge of deficient areas from the Sport Pilot knowledge test as required per §61.39 for the practical test.
SIGNED _____ DATE _____
CFI NO. _____ EXPIRATION DATE _____

PASSING THE SPORT PILOT PRACTICAL TEST

I certify that *(First name, MI, Last name)* _____,
has met the training and endorsement requirements of §§61.309, 61.311 and 61.313. I have determined him/her proficient to act as PIC of *(category/class)* _____ of light-sport aircraft.
SIGNED _____ DATE _____
PILOT CERT # _____ DPE # _____ EXP. DATE _____

ADDITIONAL SPORT PILOT ENDORSEMENTS

TAKING FLIGHT PROFICIENCY CHECK FOR AN ADDITIONAL AIRCRAFT

I certify that *(First name, MI, Last name)* _____,
has received the required training of §§61.309 and 61.311. I have determined that he/she is prepared for the *(category/class)* _____
_____ proficiency check.

SIGNED _____ DATE _____

CFI NO. _____ EXPIRATION DATE _____

PASSING FLIGHT PROFICIENCY CHECK FOR AN ADDITIONAL AIRCRAFT

I certify that *(First name, MI, Last name)* _____,
has met the training and endorsement requirements of §§61.309 and 61.311. I have determined him/her proficient to act as PIC of *(category/class)* _____
_____ of light-sport aircraft.

SIGNED _____ DATE _____

CFI NO. _____ EXPIRATION DATE _____

PRIVILEGES TO OPERATE A DIFFERENT AIRCRAFT

I certify that *(First name, MI, Last name)* _____,
has received the required training of §61.321 in a *(category/class)* _____
_____. I have determined him/her proficient to act as PIC of that light-sport aircraft.

SIGNED _____ DATE _____

CFI NO. _____ EXPIRATION DATE _____

AIRSPACE & AIRSPEED ENDORSEMENTS

I certify that *(First name, MI, Last name)* _____,
has received the required training of §61.327 in a *(make and model aircraft)* _____. I have determined him/her proficient to act as PIC of a light-sport aircraft that has a V_H greater/less than 87 knots (kts) CAS.

SIGNED _____ DATE _____

CFI NO. _____ EXPIRATION DATE _____

I certify that *(First name, MI, Last name)* _____,
has received the required training of §61.325. I have determined he/she is proficient to conduct operations in Class B, C, or D airspace, at an airport located in Class B, C, or D airspace, or to, from, through, or on an airport having an operational control tower.

SIGNED _____ DATE _____

CFI NO. _____ EXPIRATION DATE _____

I certify that *(First name, MI, Last name)* _____,
has received the training required in accordance with §61.327 in a *(make and model aircraft)* _____.
I have determined him/her proficient to act as PIC of a light-sport aircraft that has a V_H greater/less than 87 knots (kts) CAS.

SIGNED _____ DATE _____

CFI NO. _____ EXPIRATION DATE _____

RECREATIONAL PILOT ENDORSEMENTS

I certify that *(First name, MI, Last name)* _____, has received the required training of §61.97(b) and/or I have reviewed the home study curriculum and have determined that he/she is prepared for the *(name the knowledge test/aircraft category)* _____.

SIGNED _____ DATE _____

CFI NO. _____ EXPIRATION DATE _____

I certify that *(First name, MI, Last name)* _____, has received the required cross-country training of §61.101(c) and have determined that he/she is proficient in cross-country flying of part 61, subpart E.

SIGNED _____ DATE _____

CFI NO. _____ EXPIRATION DATE _____

I certify that *(First name, MI, Last name)* _____, has received the required training of §§61.98(b) and 61.99 and have determined that he/she is prepared for the *(name the practical test)* _____.

SIGNED _____ DATE _____

CFI NO. _____ EXPIRATION DATE _____

I certify that *(First name, MI, Last name)* _____, has received the required 180-day recurrent training of §61.101(f) in a *(make and model aircraft)* _____. I have determined him/her to be proficient to act as PIC of that aircraft.

SIGNED _____ DATE _____

CFI NO. _____ EXPIRATION DATE _____

I certify that *(First name, MI, Last name)* _____, has received the required training of §61.101(b) and have determined he/she is competent to operate at the *(name of airport)* _____.

SIGNED _____ DATE _____

CFI NO. _____ EXPIRATION DATE _____

I certify that *(First name, MI, Last name)* _____, has received the required training of §61.87 in a *(make and model aircraft)* _____. I have determined he/she is prepared to conduct a solo flight on *(date)* _____ under the following conditions: _____

SIGNED _____ DATE _____

CFI NO. _____ EXPIRATION DATE _____

PRIVATE PILOT ENDORSEMENTS	**COMMERCIAL PILOT ENDORSEMENTS**
I certify that *(First name, MI, Last name)* _____, has received the required training of §61.105 and/or I have reviewed the home study curriculum and have determined he/she is prepared for the *(name the knowledge test/aircraft category)* _____. SIGNED _____ DATE _____ CFI NO. _____ EXPIRATION DATE _____	I certify that *(First name, MI, Last name)* _____, has received the required training of §61.125 and/or I have reviewed the home study curriculum and have determined that he/she is prepared for the *(name the knowledge test/aircraft category)* _____. SIGNED _____ DATE _____ CFI NO. _____ EXPIRATION DATE _____
I certify that *(First name, MI, Last name)* _____, has received the required training of §§61.107 and 61.109 and have determined he/she is prepared for the *(name the practical test)* _____. SIGNED _____ DATE _____ CFI NO. _____ EXPIRATION DATE _____	I certify that *(First name, MI, Last name)* _____, has received the required training of §§61.127 and 61.129 and have determined he/she is prepared for the *(name the practical test)* _____. SIGNED _____ DATE _____ CFI NO. _____ EXPIRATION DATE _____
I certify that *(First name, MI, Last name)* _____, has received the training as required by §61.39(a)(6)(i) within the preceding two calendar months and have determined that he/she is prepared for the *(name the practical test)* _____ and has demonstrated satisfactory knowledge of subject areas shown to be deficient on his/her Airman Knowledge Test as required by §61.39(a)(6)(iii). SIGNED _____ DATE _____ CFI NO. _____ EXPIRATION DATE _____	I certify that *(First name, MI, Last name)* _____, has received the training as required by §61.39(a)(6)(i) within the preceding two calendar months and have determined that he/she is prepared for the *(name the practical test)* _____ and has demonstrated satisfactory knowledge of subject areas shown to be deficient on his/her Airman Knowledge Test as required by §61.39(a)(6)(iii). SIGNED _____ DATE _____ CFI NO. _____ EXPIRATION DATE _____

INSTRUMENT RATING ENDORSEMENTS	**INSTRUMENT PROFICIENCY**
I certify that *(First name, MI, Last name)* _____, has received the required training of §61.65(b) and/or I have reviewed the home study curriculum and have determined that he/she is prepared for the *(name the knowledge test/aircraft category)* _____. SIGNED _____ DATE _____ CFI NO. _____ EXPIRATION DATE _____	I certify that *(First name, MI, Last name)* _____, *(pilot certificate)* _____, *(certificate number)* _____, has satisfactorily completed the instrument proficiency check required in §61.57(d) in a *(make and model of aircraft)* _____ on *(date)* _____. SIGNED _____ DATE _____ CFI NO. _____ EXPIRATION DATE _____
I certify that *(First name, MI, Last name)* _____, has received the required training of §61.65(c) and (d) and have determined he/she is prepared for the *(name of the practical test)* _____. SIGNED _____ DATE _____ CFI NO. _____ EXPIRATION DATE _____	I certify that *(First name, MI, Last name)* _____, *(pilot certificate)* _____, *(certificate number)* _____, has satisfactorily completed the instrument proficiency check required in §61.57(d) in a *(make and model of aircraft)* _____ on *(date)* _____. SIGNED _____ DATE _____ CFI NO. _____ EXPIRATION DATE _____
I certify that *(First name, MI, Last name)* _____, has received the training as required by §61.39(a)(6)(i) within the preceding two calendar months and have determined that he/she is prepared for the *(name the practical test)* _____ and has demonstrated satisfactory knowledge of subject areas shown to be deficient on his/her Airman Knowledge Test as required by §61.39(a)(6)(iii). SIGNED _____ DATE _____ CFI NO. _____ EXPIRATION DATE _____	I certify that *(First name, MI, Last name)* _____, *(pilot certificate)* _____, *(certificate number)* _____, has satisfactorily completed the instrument proficiency check required in §61.57(d) in a *(make and model of aircraft)* _____ on *(date)* _____. SIGNED _____ DATE _____ CFI NO. _____ EXPIRATION DATE _____

FLIGHT AND GROUND INSTRUCTOR ENDORSEMENTS

I certify that *(First name, MI, Last name)* _____,
has received the required fundamentals of instruction training of §61.185(a)(1).

SIGNED _____ DATE _____
CFI NO. _____ EXPIRATION DATE _____

I certify that *(First name, MI, Last name)* _____
has received the required training of §61.183(i) and have determined that he/she is competent and proficient in instructional skills for training stall awareness, spin entry, spins, and spin recovery procedures. *(Required of flight instructor applicants for the airplane and glider ratings only.)*

SIGNED _____ DATE _____
CFI NO. _____ EXPIRATION DATE _____

I certify that *(First name, MI, Last name)* _____,
has received the required training of §61.187(b) and/or I have reviewed the home study curriculum and have determined he/she is prepared for the *(name the knowledge test/aircraft category)* _____.

SIGNED _____ DATE _____
CFI NO. _____ EXPIRATION DATE _____

I certify that *(First name, MI, Last name)* _____
has demonstrated satisfactory proficiency on the appropriate ground instructor knowledge and training subjects of §61.213(a)(3) and (a)(4).

SIGNED _____ DATE _____
CFI NO. _____ EXPIRATION DATE _____

I certify that *(First name, MI, Last name)* _____,
has received the required CFII training of §61.187(b)(7) and have determined he/she is prepared for the *(name of practical test)* _____.

SIGNED _____ DATE _____
CFI NO. _____ EXPIRATION DATE _____

I certify that *(First name, MI, Last name)* _____,
has received the training as required by §61.39(a)(6)(i) within the preceding two calendar months and have determined that he/she is prepared for the *(name the practical test)* _____ and has demonstrated satisfactory knowledge of subject areas shown to be deficient on his/her Airman Knowledge Test as required by §61.39(a)(6)(iii).

SIGNED _____ DATE _____
CFI NO. _____ EXPIRATION DATE _____

ADDITIONAL ENDORSEMENTS

COMPLEX AIRPLANE

I certify that *(First name, MI, Last name)* _____,
(pilot certificate) _____, *(certificate number)* _____,
has received the required training of §61.31(e) in a *(make and model of complex airplane)* _____. I have determined that he/she is proficient in the operation and systems of a complex airplane.

SIGNED _____ DATE _____
CFI NO. _____ EXPIRATION DATE _____

HIGH-PERFORMANCE AIRPLANE

I certify that *(First name, MI, Last name)* _____,
(pilot certificate) _____, *(certificate number)* _____,
has received the required training of §61.31(f) in a *(make and model of high performance airplane)* _____
I have determined that he/she is proficient in the operation and systems of a high performance airplane.

SIGNED _____ DATE _____
CFI NO. _____ EXPIRATION DATE _____

HIGH ALTITUDE

I certify that *(First name, MI, Last name)* _____,
(pilot certificate) _____, *(certificate number)* _____,
has received the required training of §61.31(g) in a *(make and model of pressurized aircraft)* _____.
I have determined that he/she is proficient in the operation and systems of a pressurized aircraft.

SIGNED _____ DATE _____
CFI NO. _____ EXPIRATION DATE _____

TAILWHEEL

I certify that *(First name, MI, Last name)* _____,
(pilot certificate) _____, *(certificate number)* _____,
has received the required training of §61.31(i) in a *(make and model of tailwheel airplane)* _____. I have determined that he/she is proficient in the operation of a tailwheel airplane.

SIGNED _____ DATE _____
CFI NO. _____ EXPIRATION DATE _____

TYPE RATING

I certify that *(First name, MI, Last name)* _____,
has received the training as required by §61.31(d)(3) to serve as a PIC in a *(category and class of aircraft)* _____. I have determined that he/she is prepared to serve as PIC in that *(make and model of aircraft)* _____

SIGNED _____ DATE _____
CFI NO. _____ EXPIRATION DATE _____

ADDED RATING

I certify that *(First name, MI, Last name)* _____,
(pilot certificate) _____, *(certificate number)* _____,
has received the required training for an additional *(name the aircraft category/class rating)* _____ . I have determined that he/she is prepared for the *(name the practical test)* _____ for the addition of a *(name the aircraft category/class rating)* _____

SIGNED _____ DATE _____
CFI NO. _____ EXPIRATION DATE _____

FLIGHT REVIEW

I certify that *(First name, MI, Last name)* _____,
(pilot certificate) _____, *(certificate number)* _____,
has satisfactorily completed the flight review required in §61.56(a) on *(date)* _____.

SIGNED _____ DATE _____
CFI NO. _____ EXPIRATION DATE _____

I certify that *(First name, MI, Last name)* _____,
(pilot certificate) _____, *(certificate number)* _____,
has satisfactorily completed the flight review required in §61.56(a) on *(date)* _____.

SIGNED _____ DATE _____
CFI NO. _____ EXPIRATION DATE _____

I certify that *(First name, MI, Last name)* _____,
(pilot certificate) _____, *(certificate number)* _____,
has satisfactorily completed the flight review required in §61.56(a) on *(date)* _____.

SIGNED _____ DATE _____
CFI NO. _____ EXPIRATION DATE _____

I certify that *(First name, MI, Last name)* _____,
(pilot certificate) _____, *(certificate number)* _____,
has satisfactorily completed the flight review required in §61.56(a) on *(date)* _____.

SIGNED _____ DATE _____
CFI NO. _____ EXPIRATION DATE _____

I certify that *(First name, MI, Last name)* _____,
(pilot certificate) _____, *(certificate number)* _____,
has satisfactorily completed the flight review required in §61.56(a) on *(date)* _____.

SIGNED _____ DATE _____
CFI NO. _____ EXPIRATION DATE _____

I certify that *(First name, MI, Last name)* _____,
(pilot certificate) _____, *(certificate number)* _____,
has satisfactorily completed the flight review required in §61.56(a) on *(date)* _____.

SIGNED _____ DATE _____
CFI NO. _____ EXPIRATION DATE _____